The Tangled Webs We Weave

MAZES PUZZLE FOR ADULTS

ActivityCrusades

Published by Speedy Publishing Canada Limited

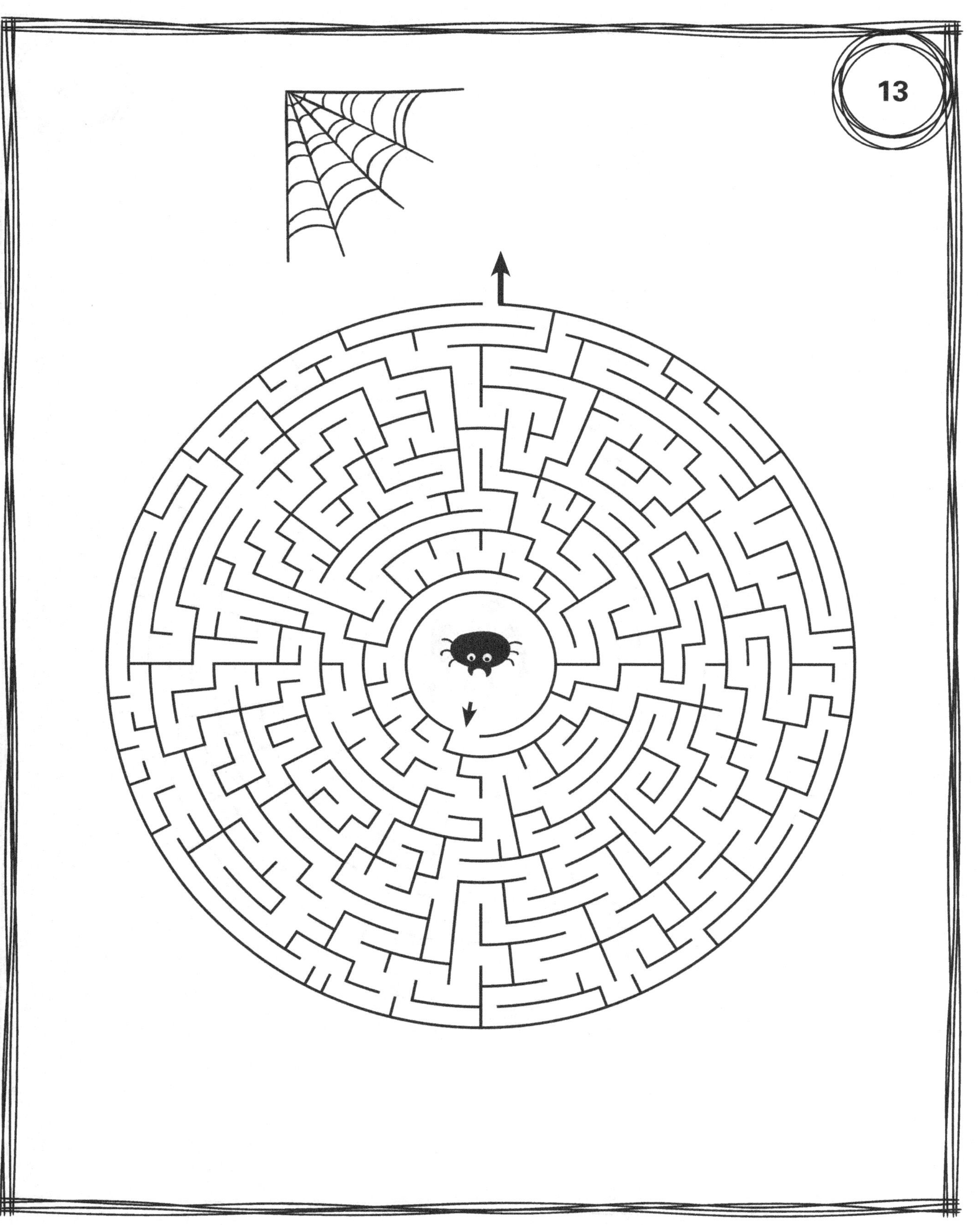

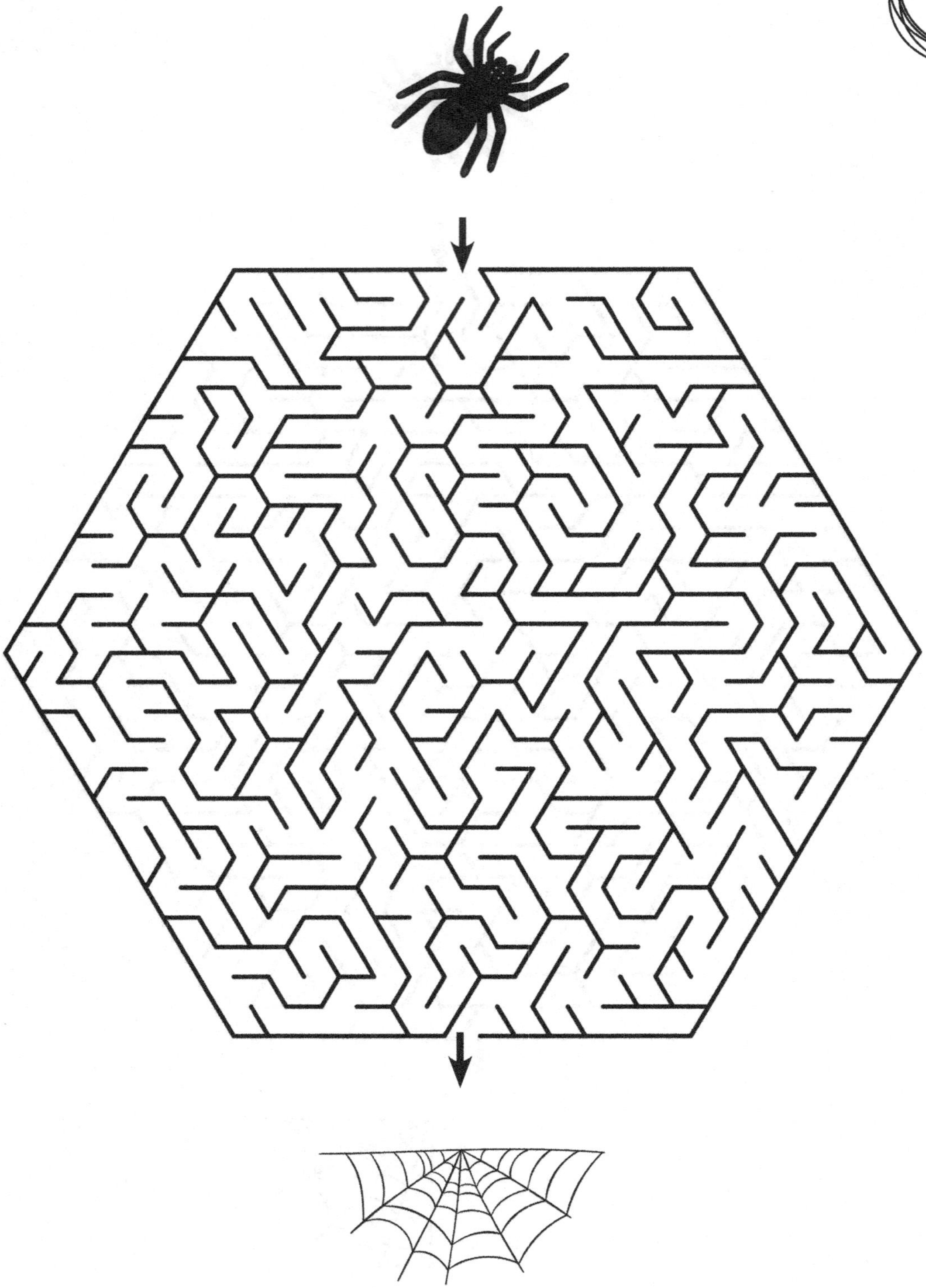

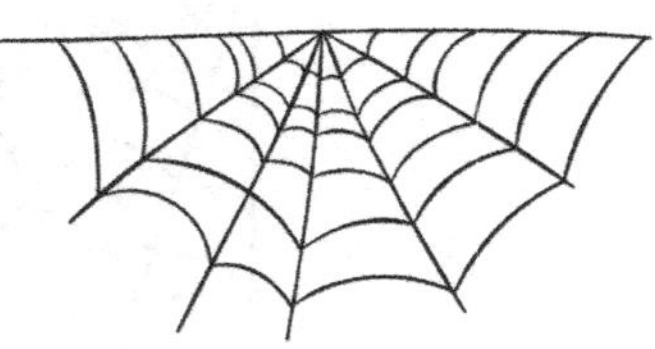

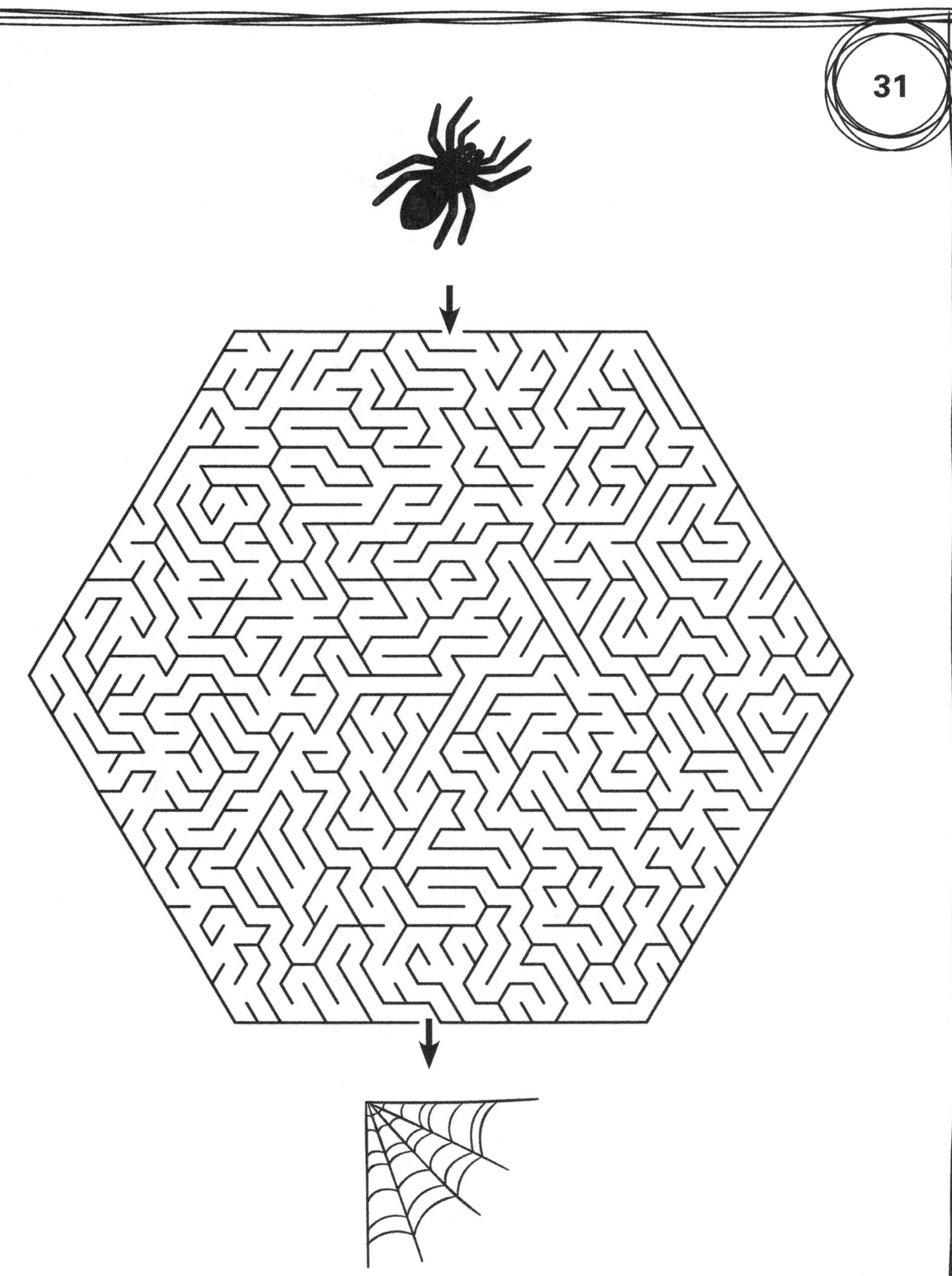

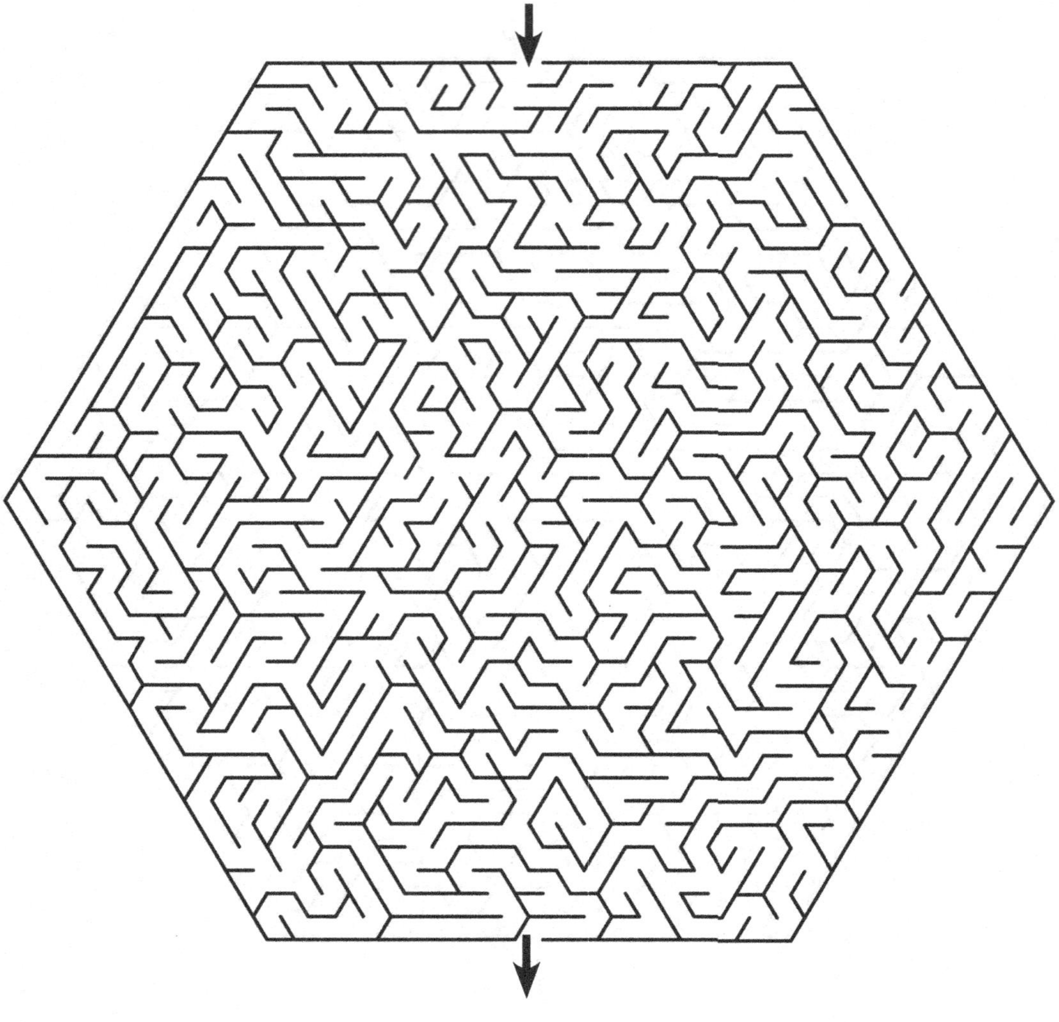

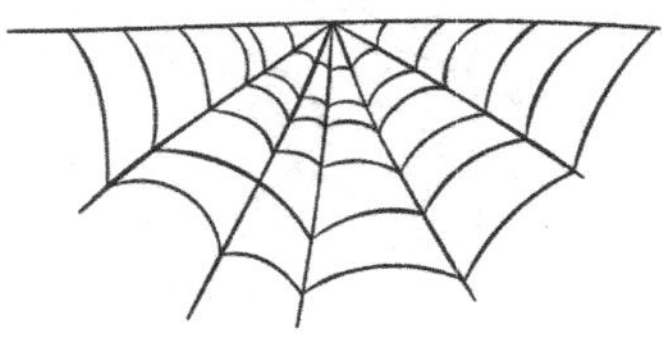

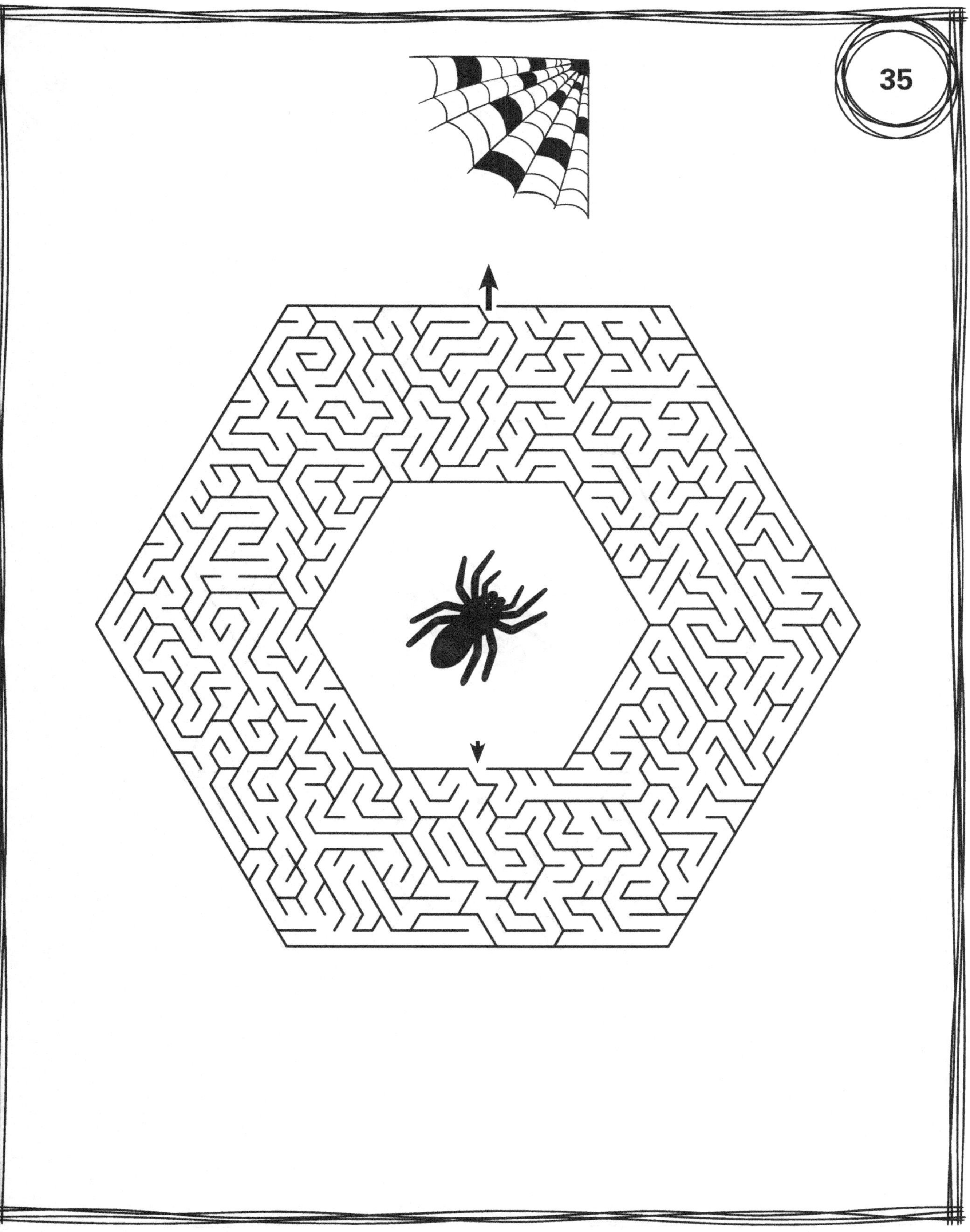

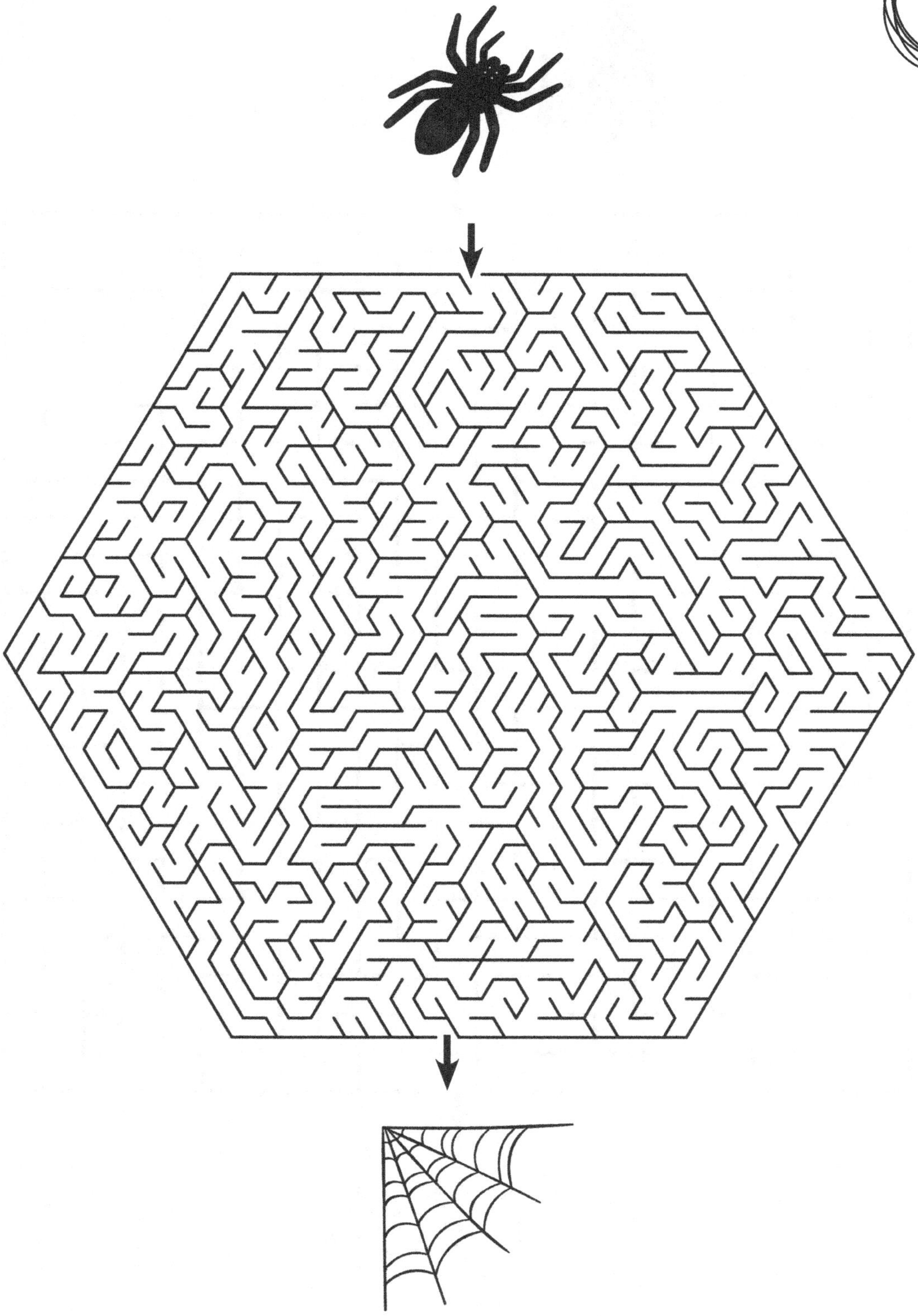

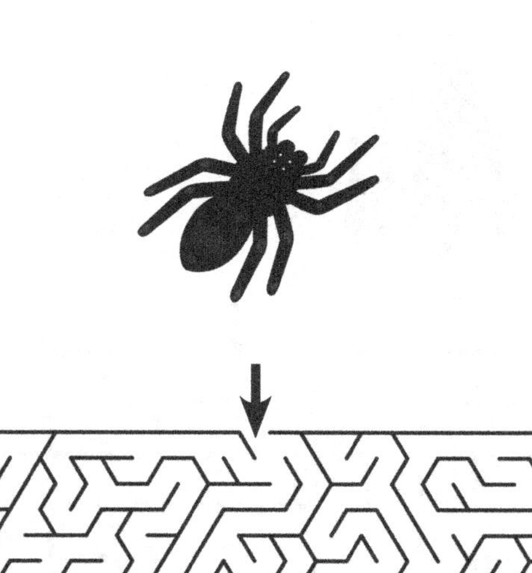

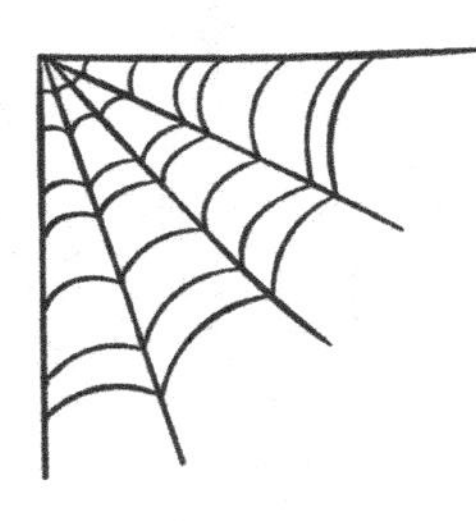

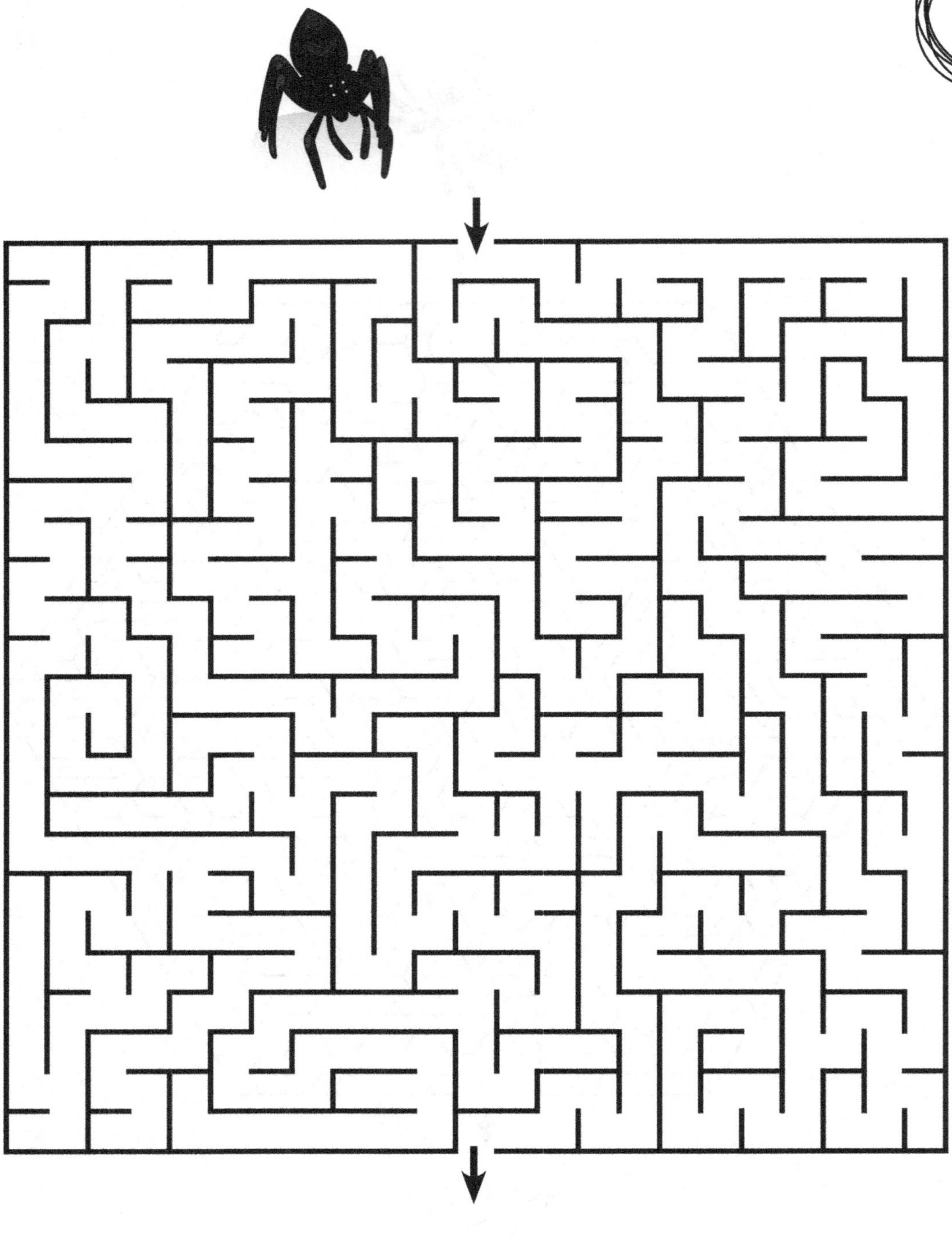

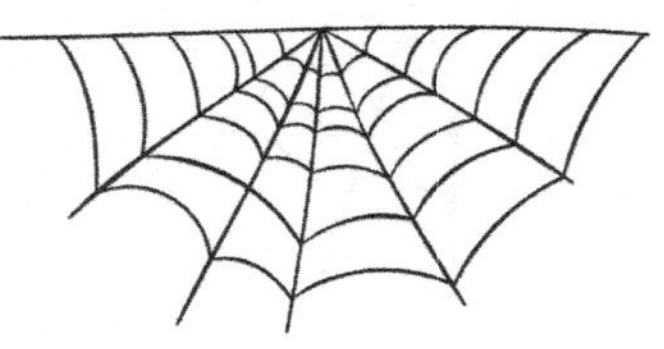

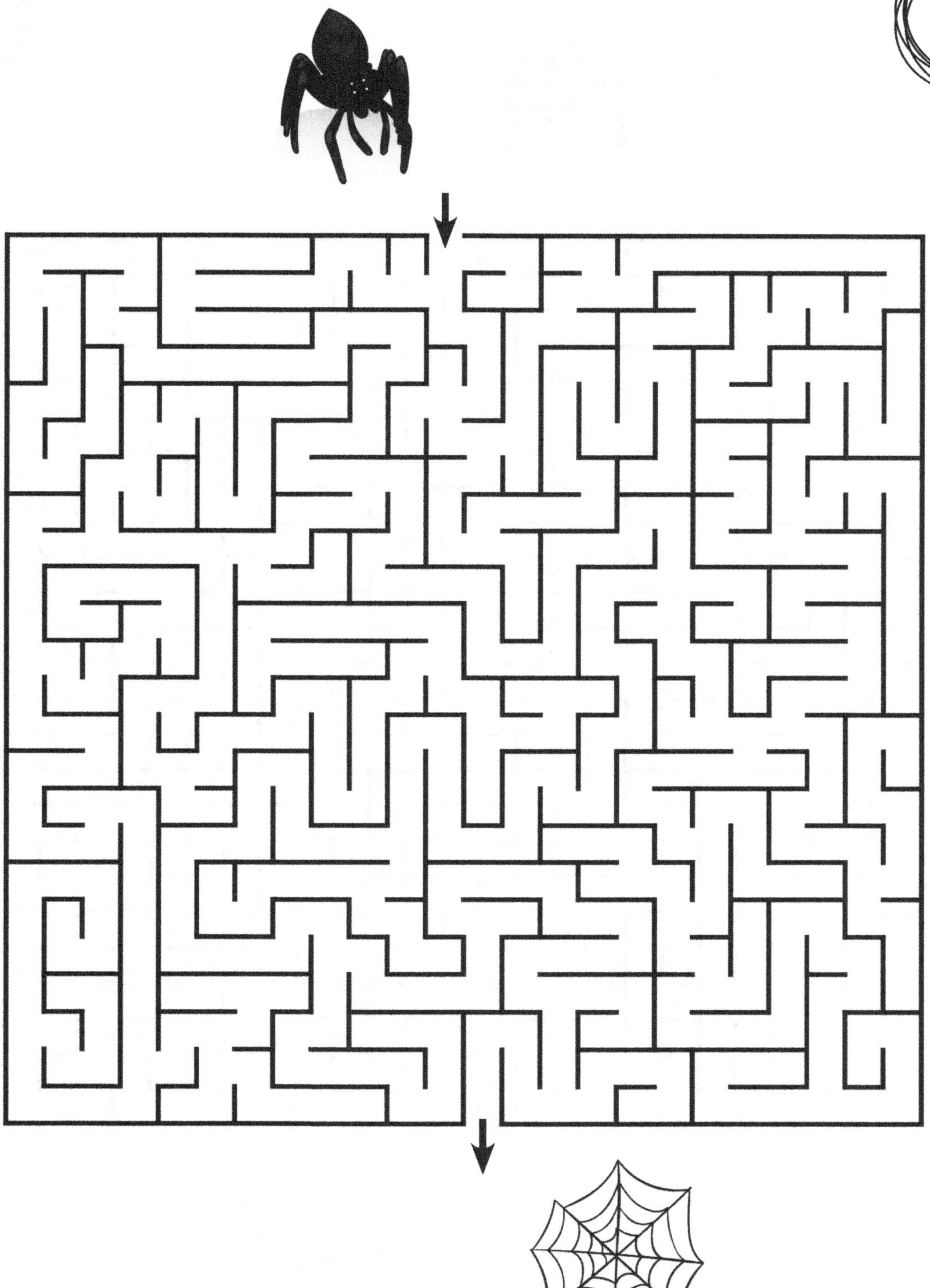

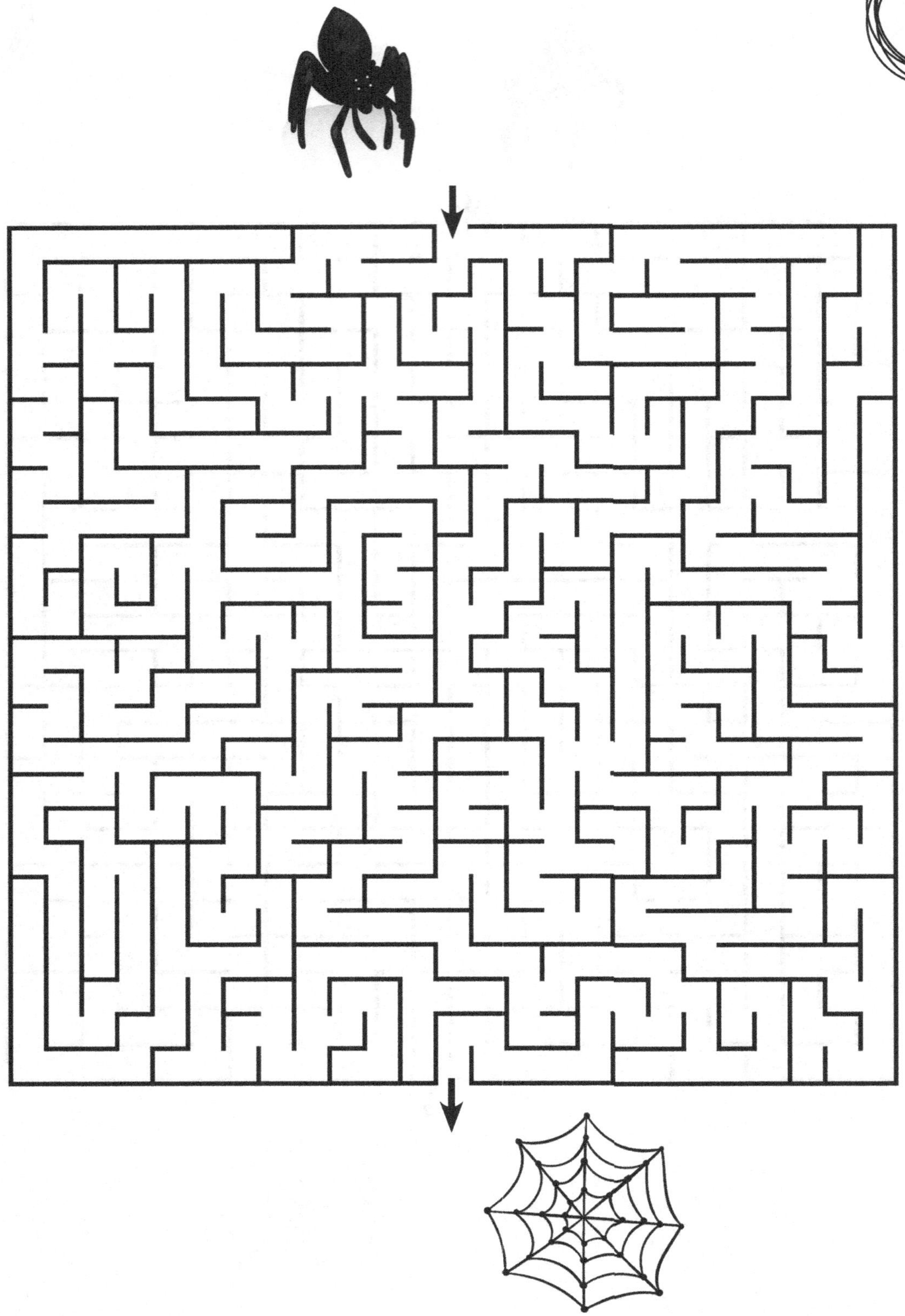

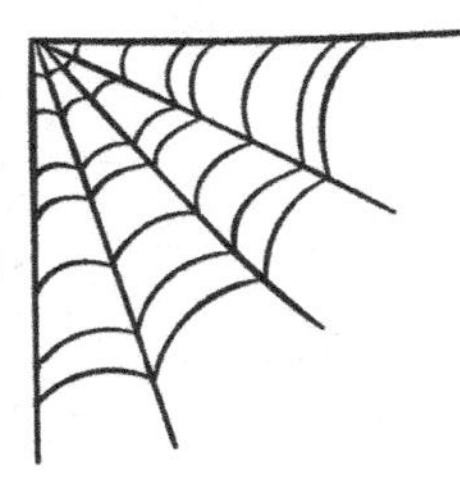

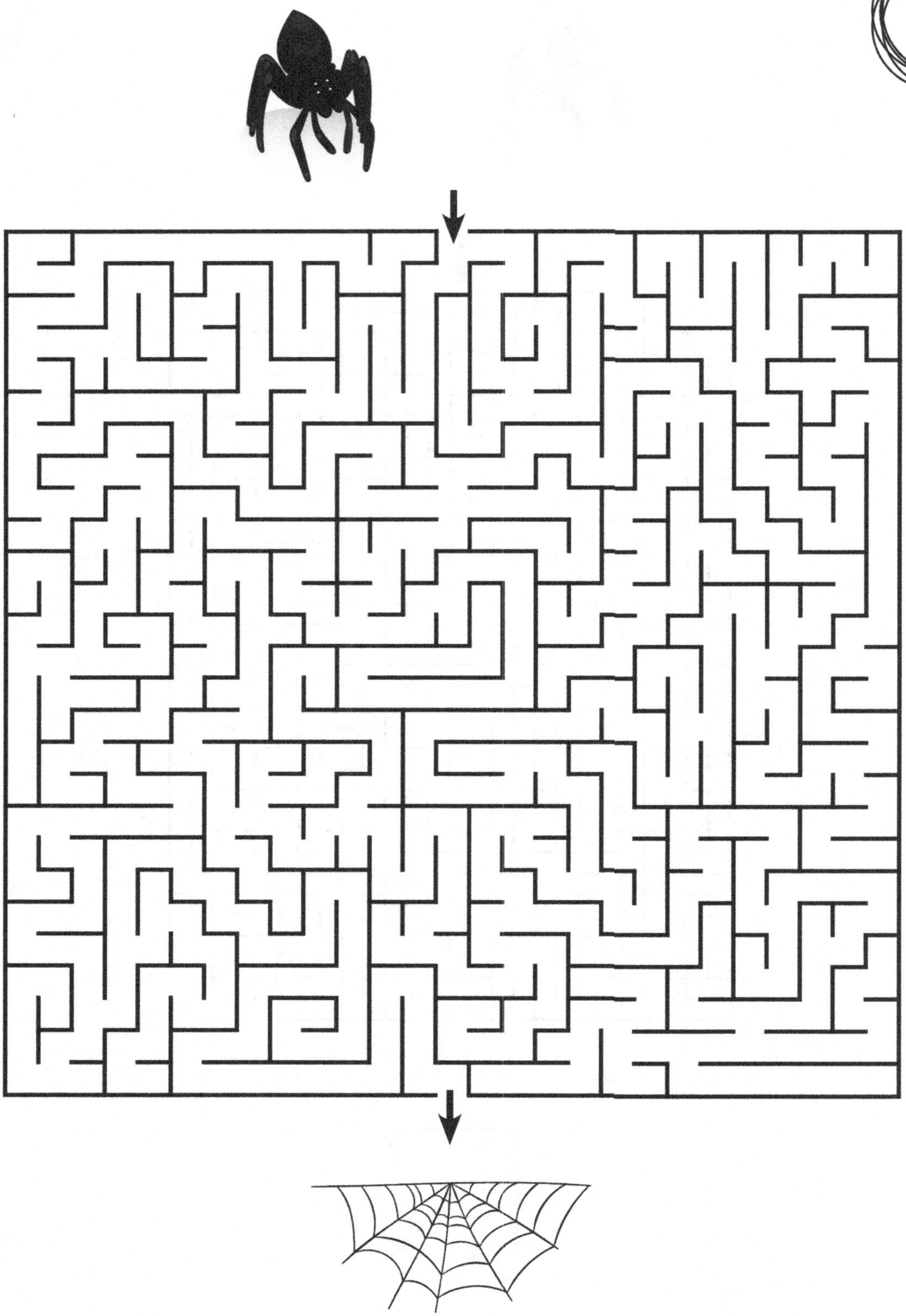

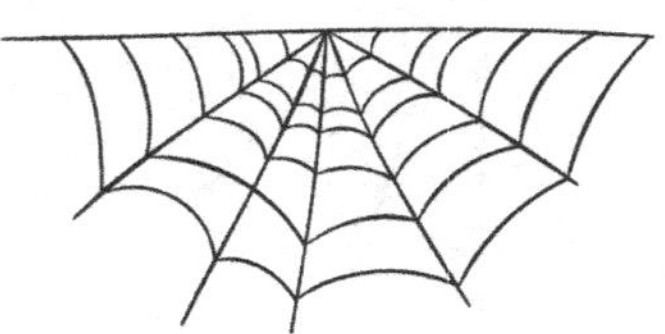

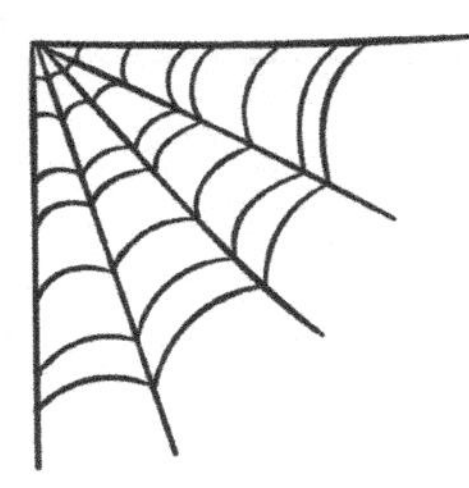

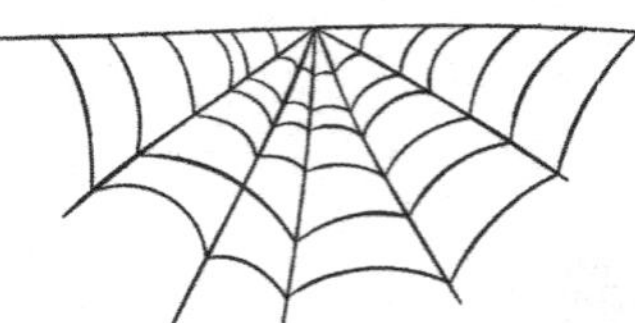

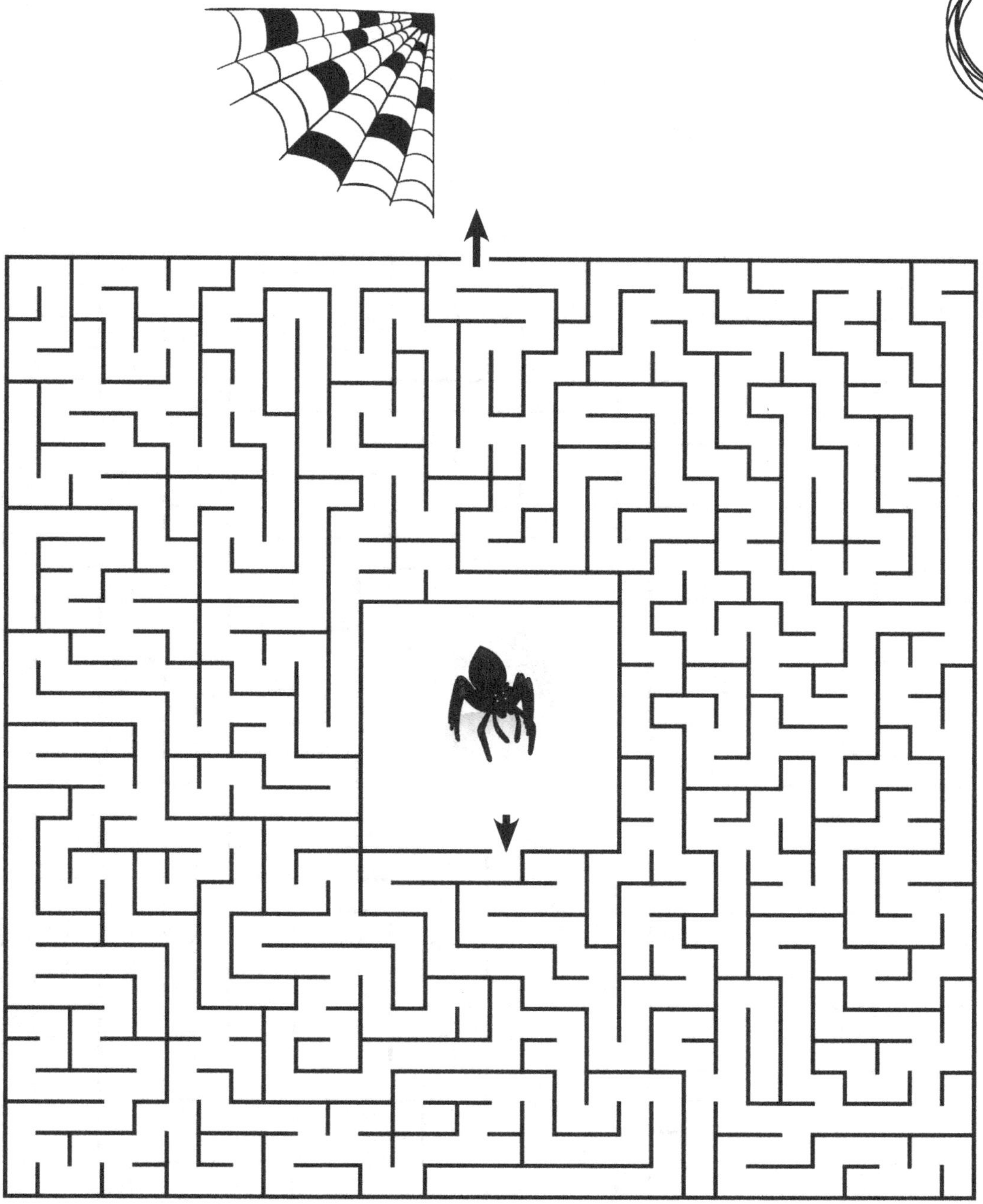

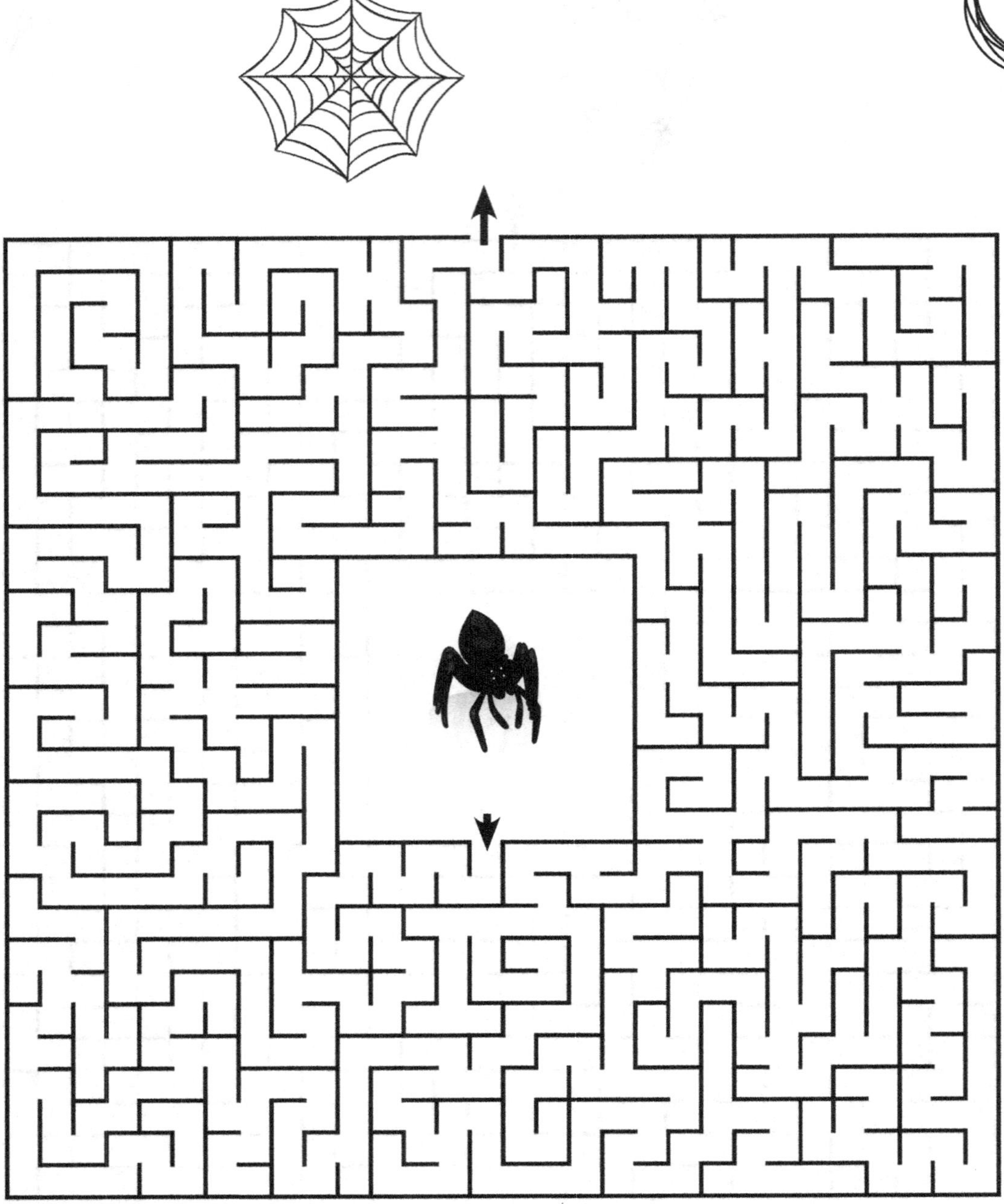

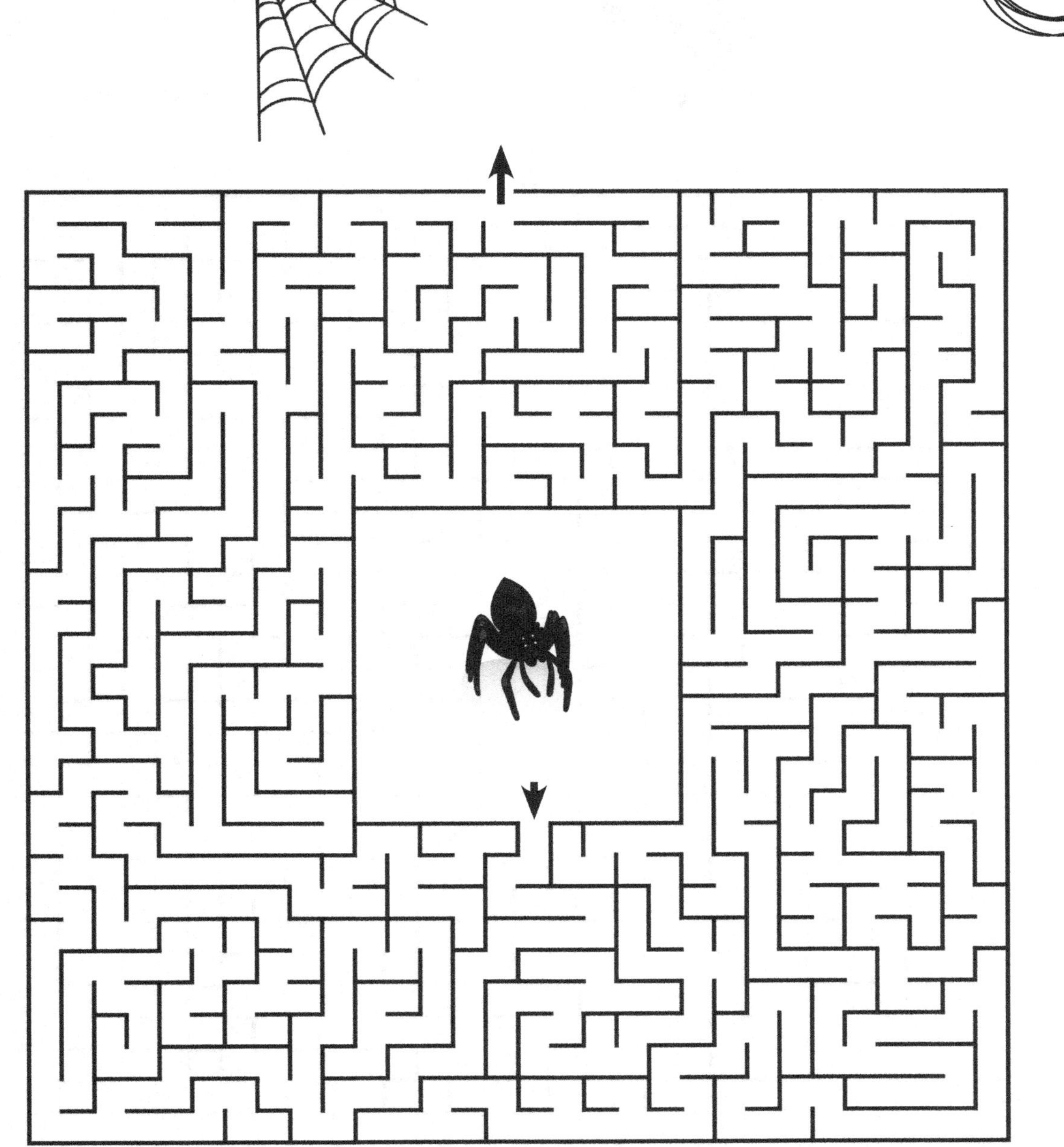

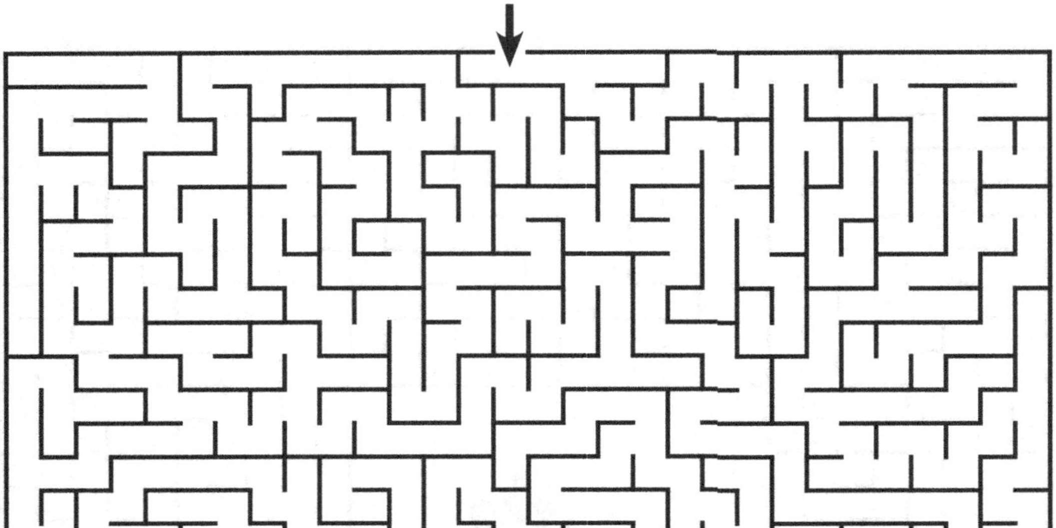

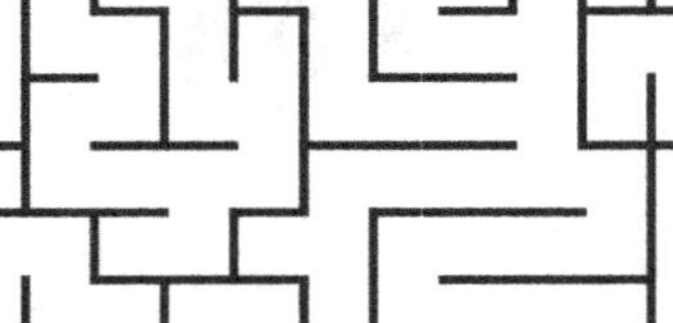

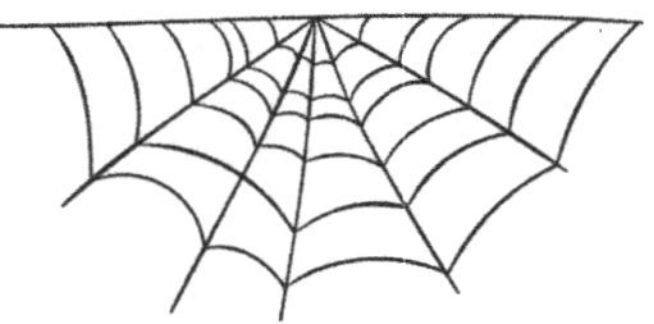

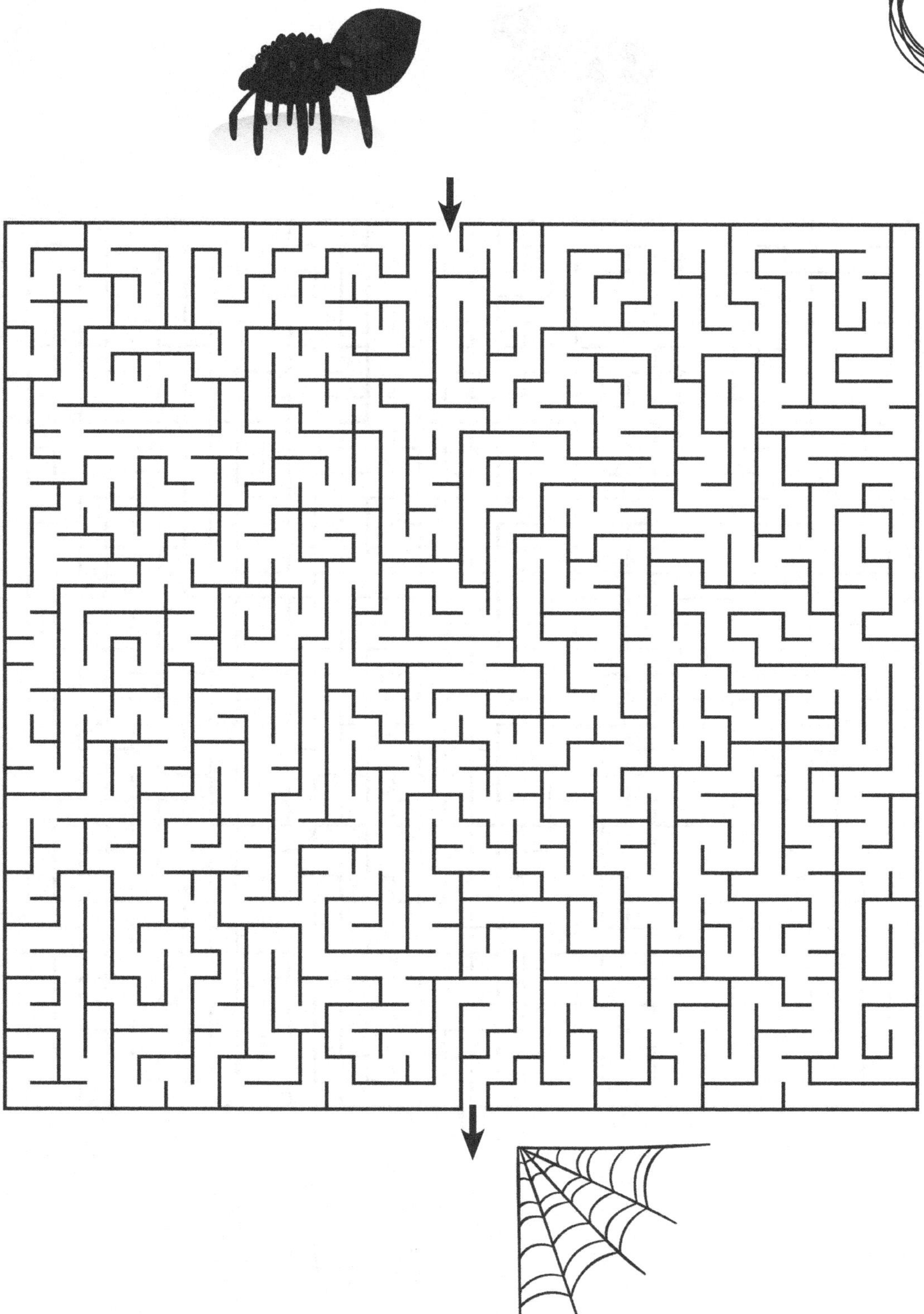

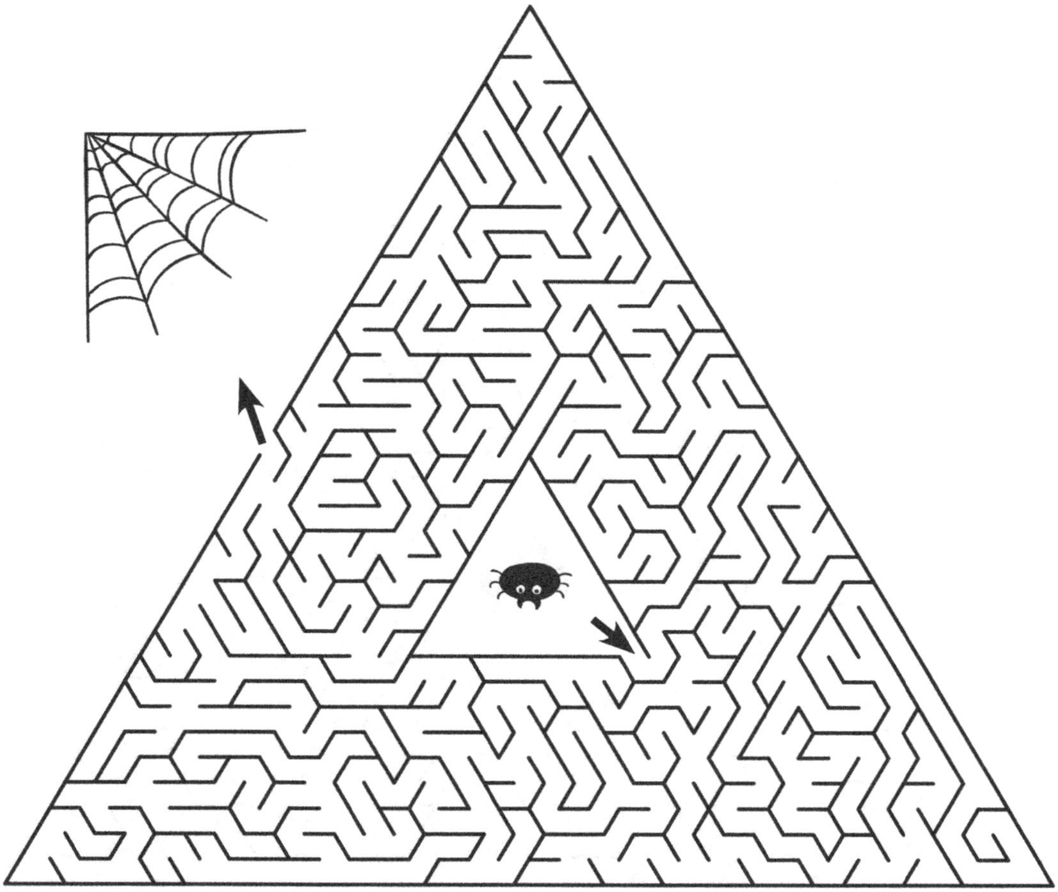

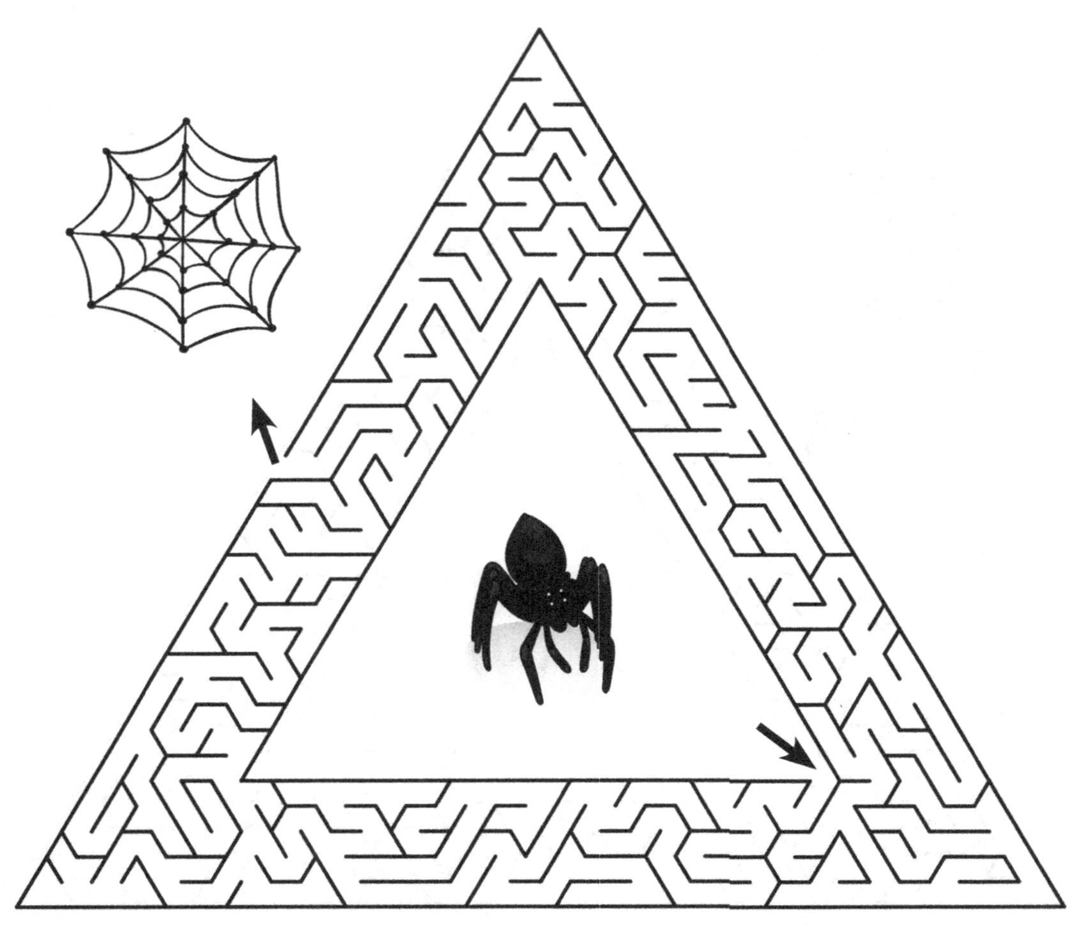

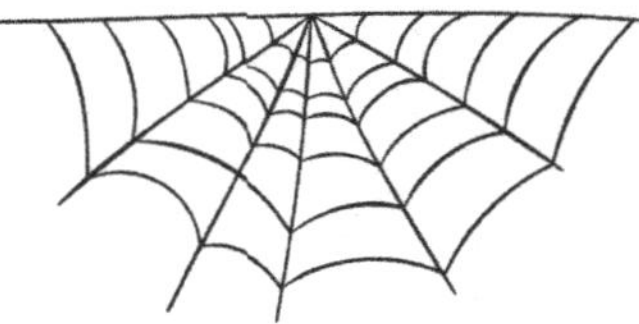

1
2
3
4

5

6

7

8

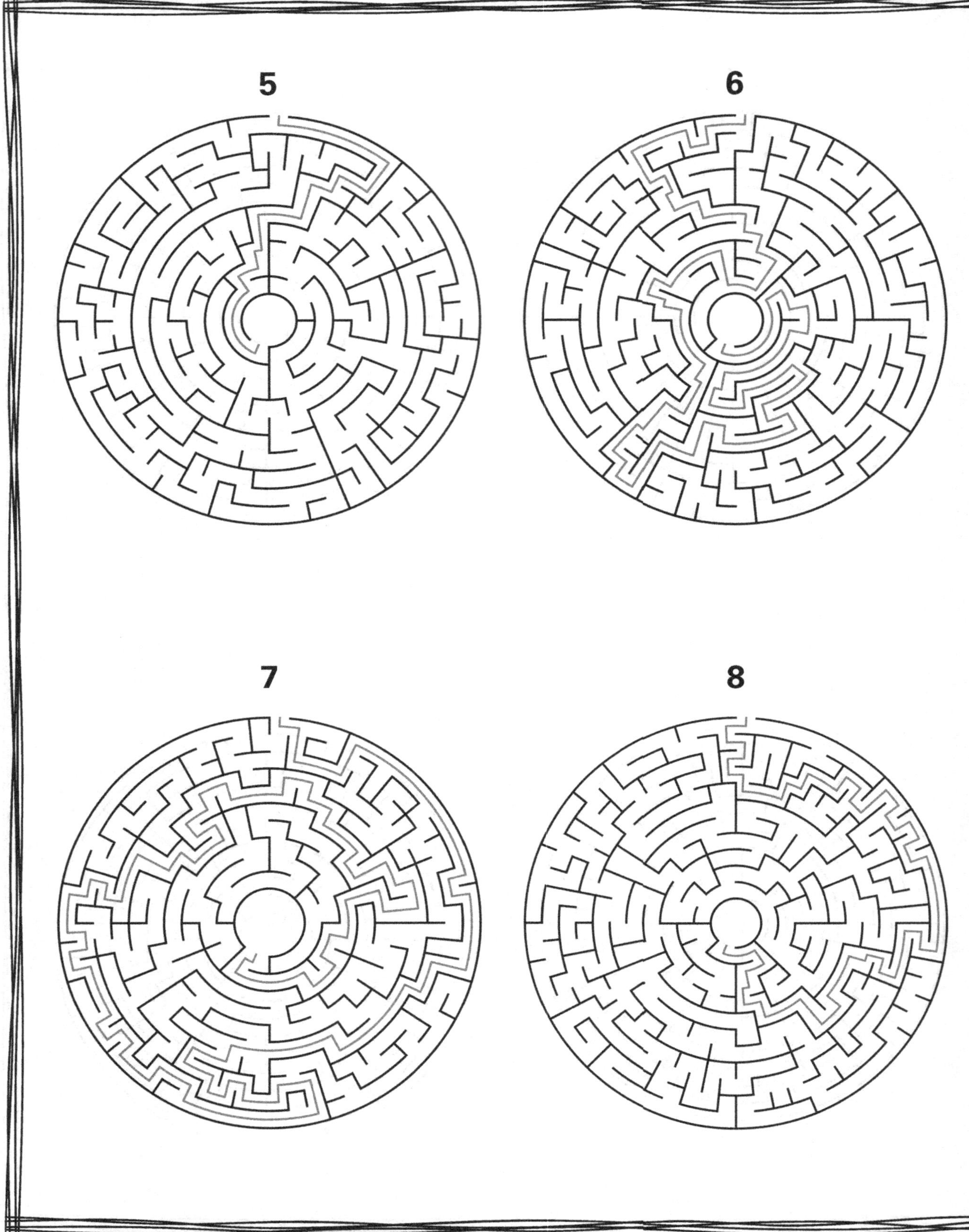

9

10

11

12

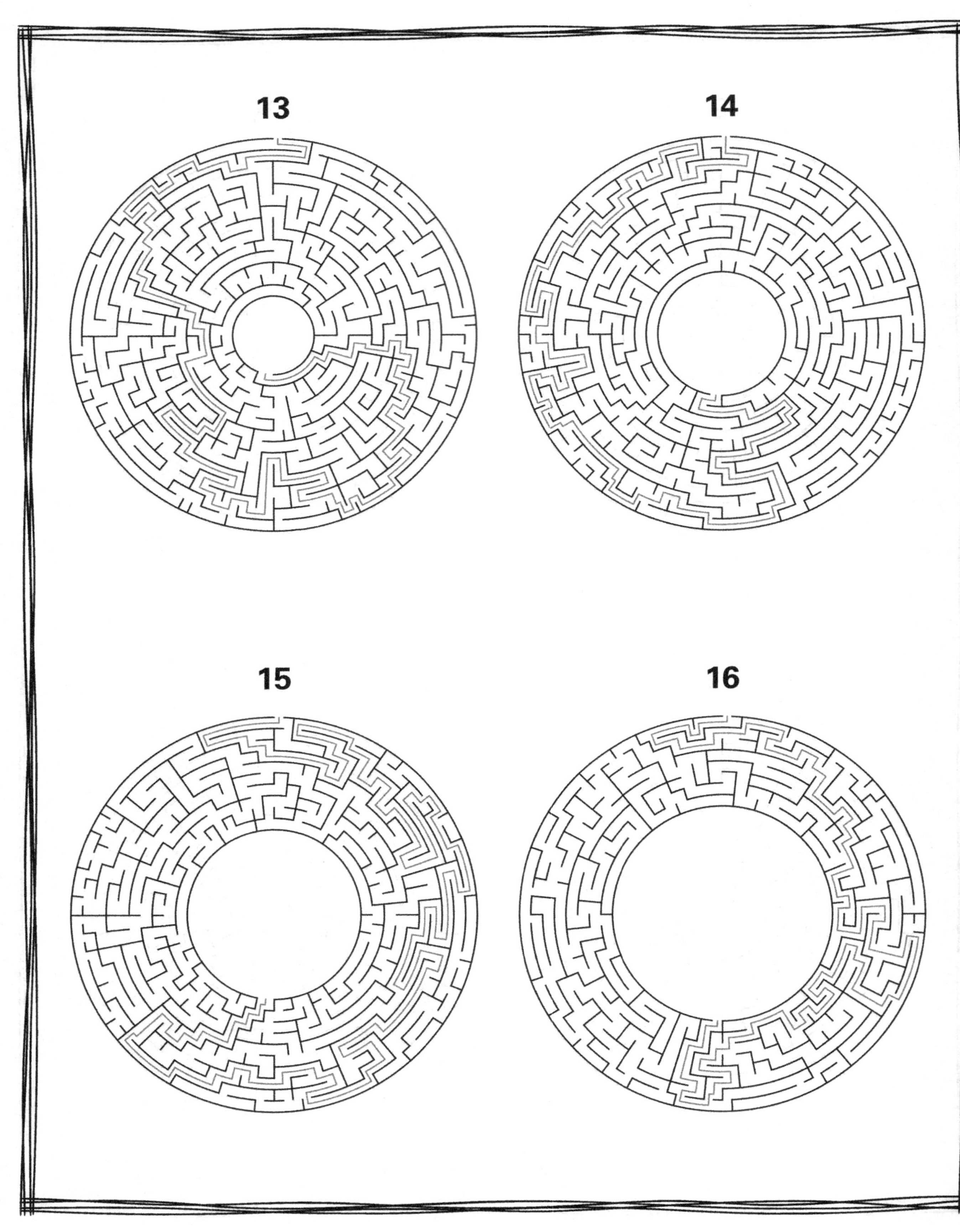

13
14
15
16

17
18
19
20

21

22

23

24

25

26

27

28

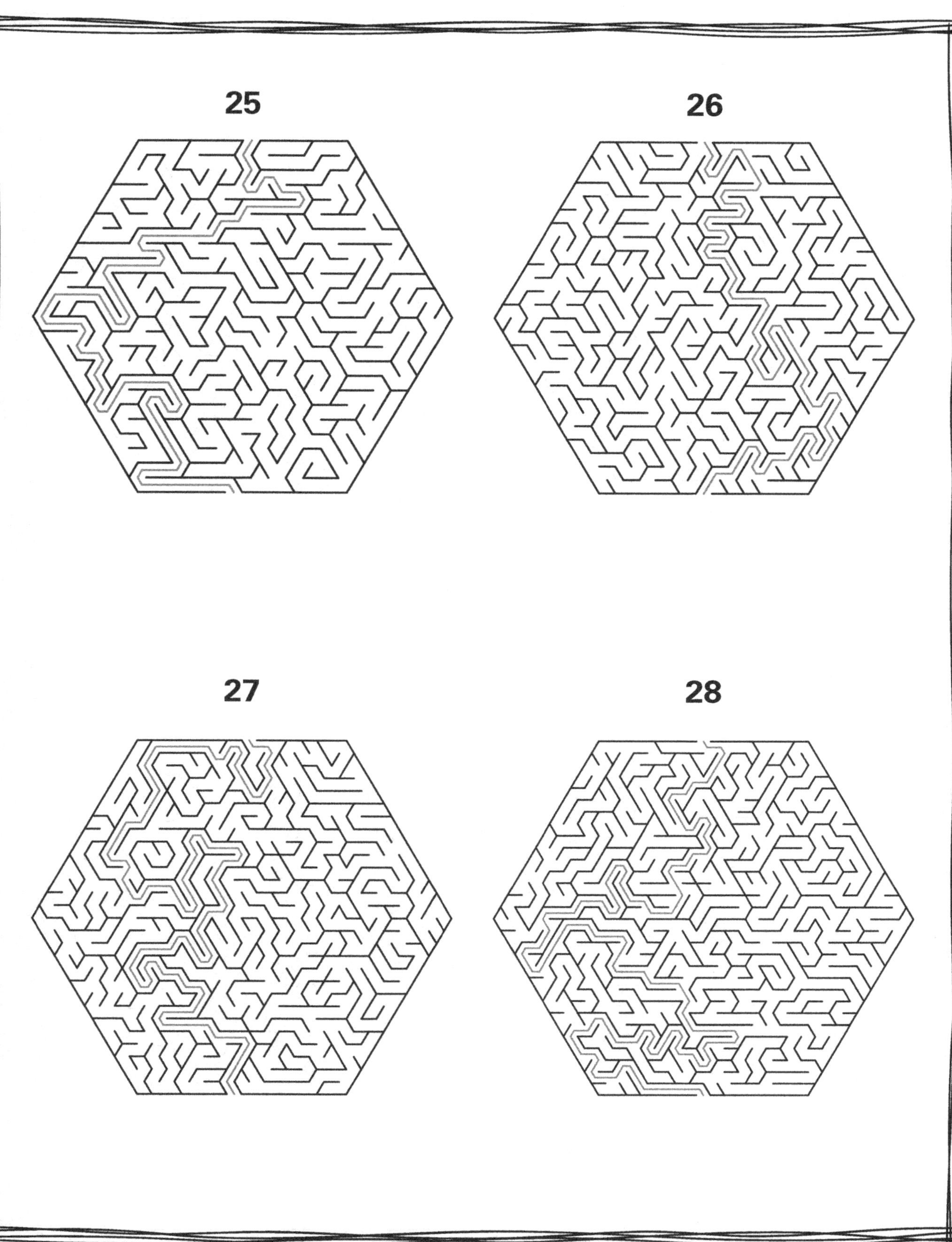

29

30

31

32

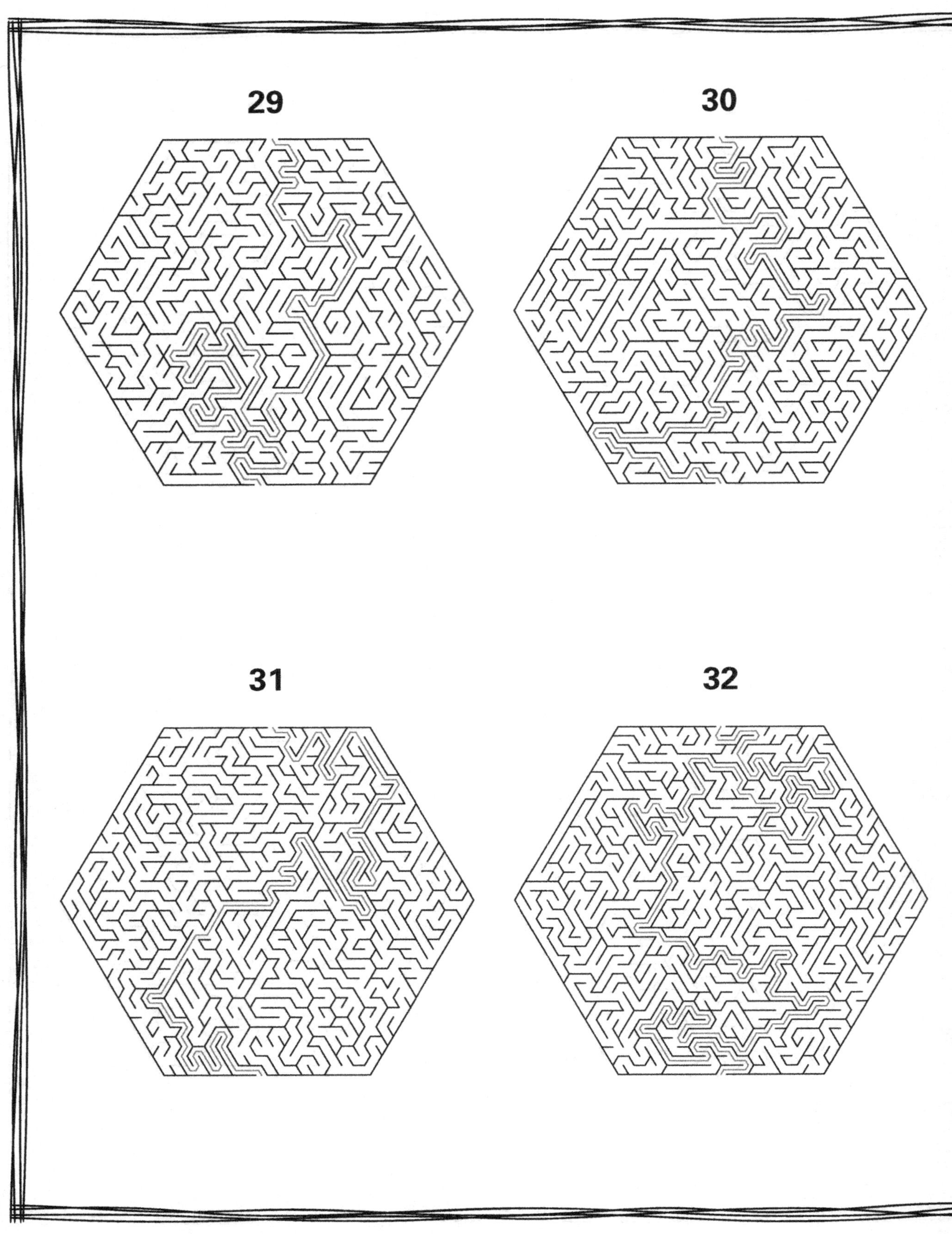

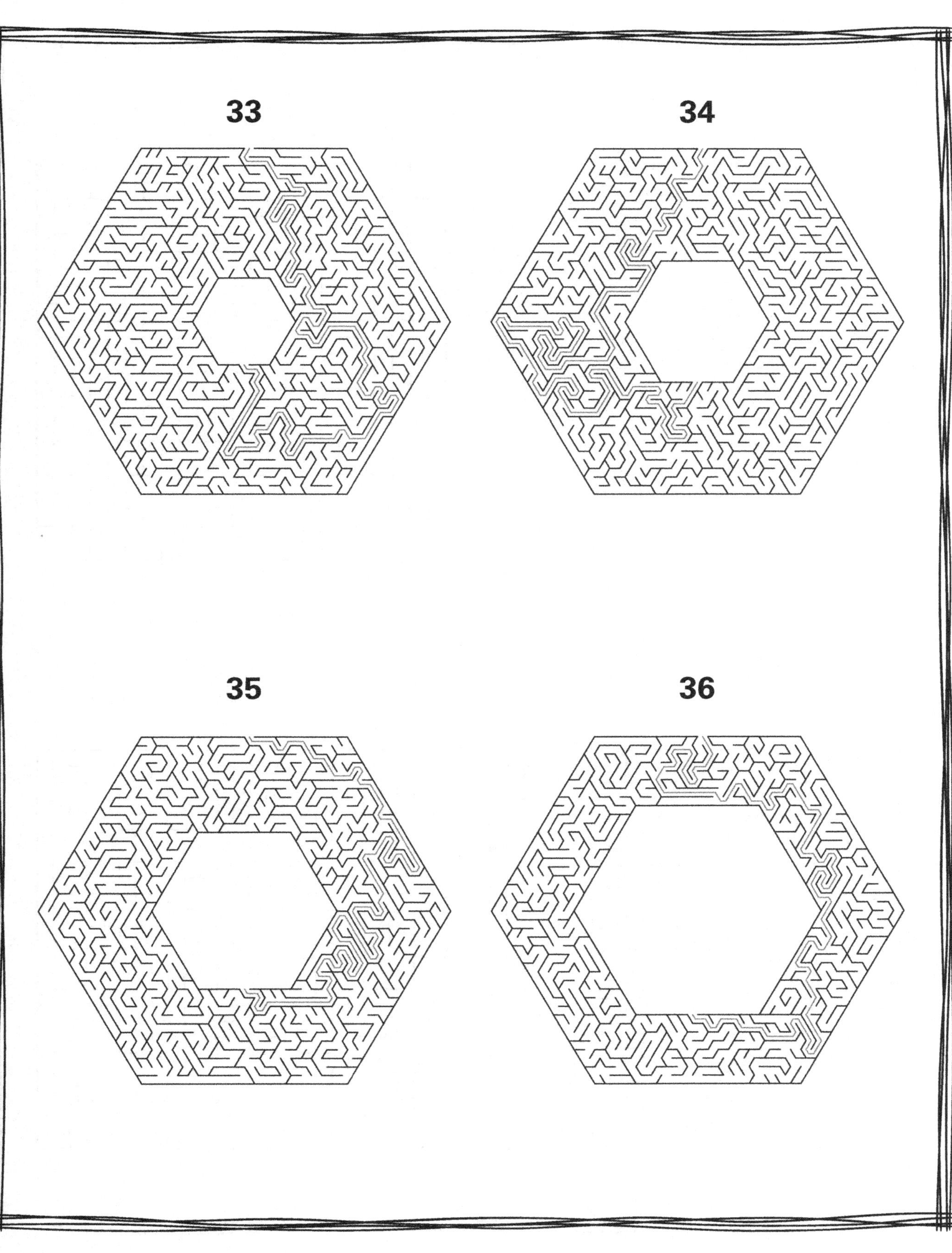
33
34
35
36

37

38

39

40

41

42

43

44

45

46

47

48

49

50

51

52

53

54

55

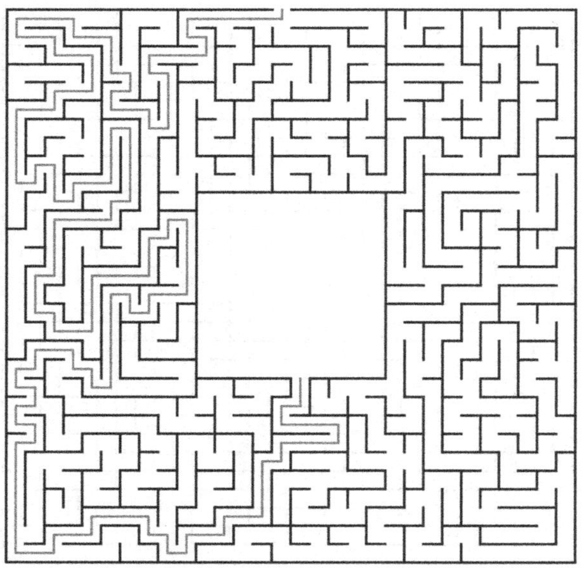

56

57

58

59

60

61

62

63

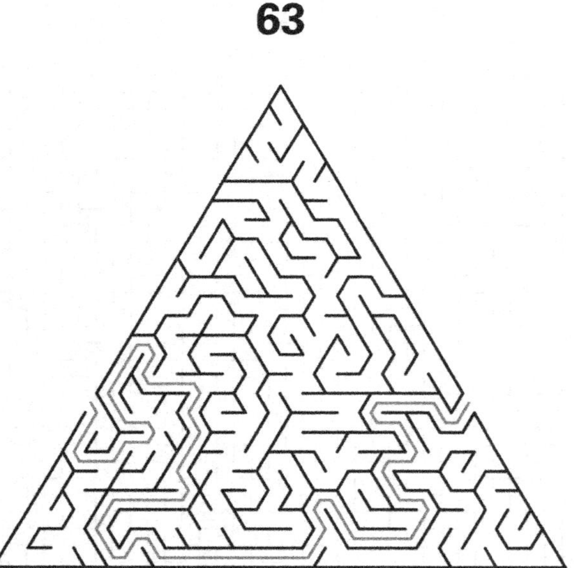

64

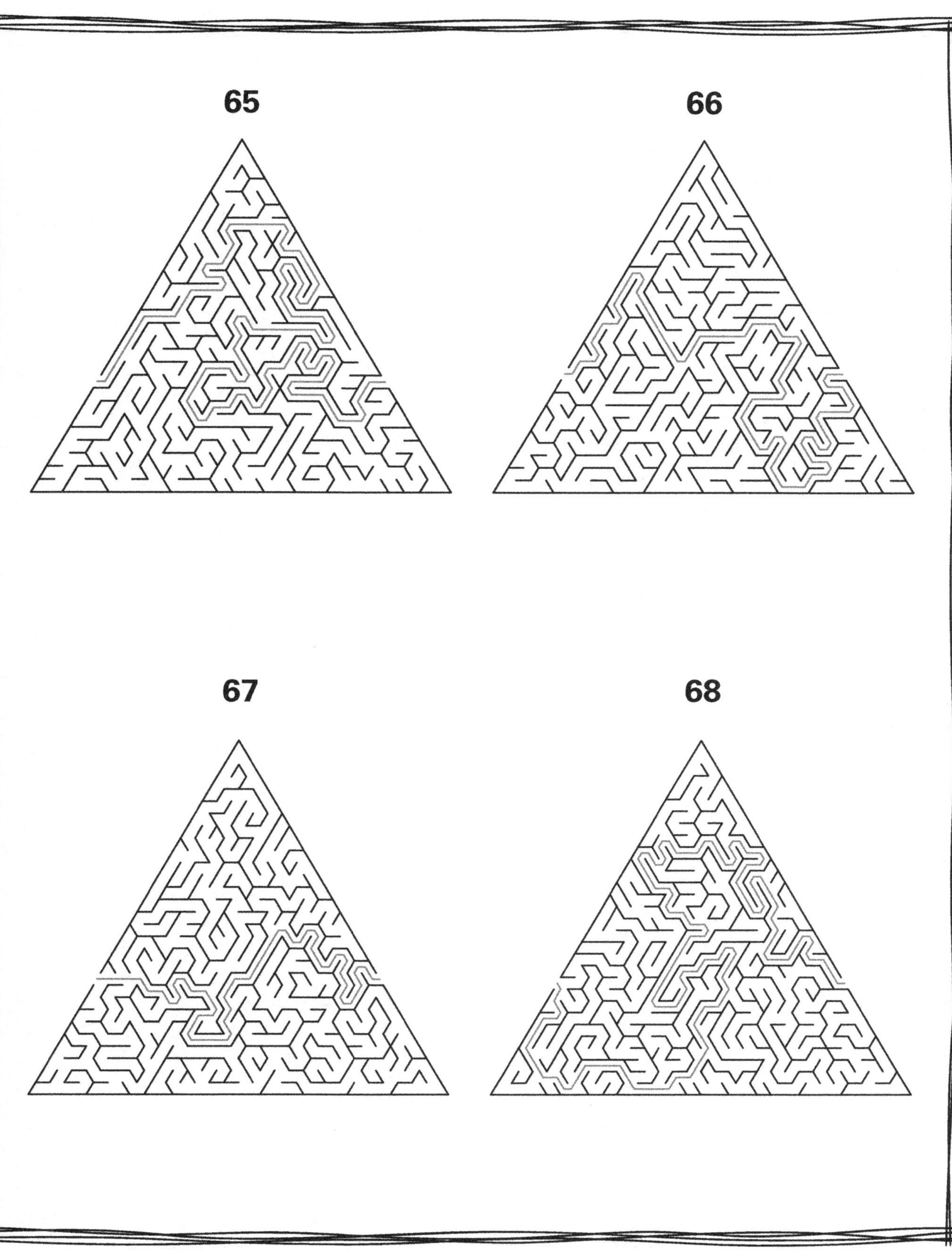
65
66
67
68

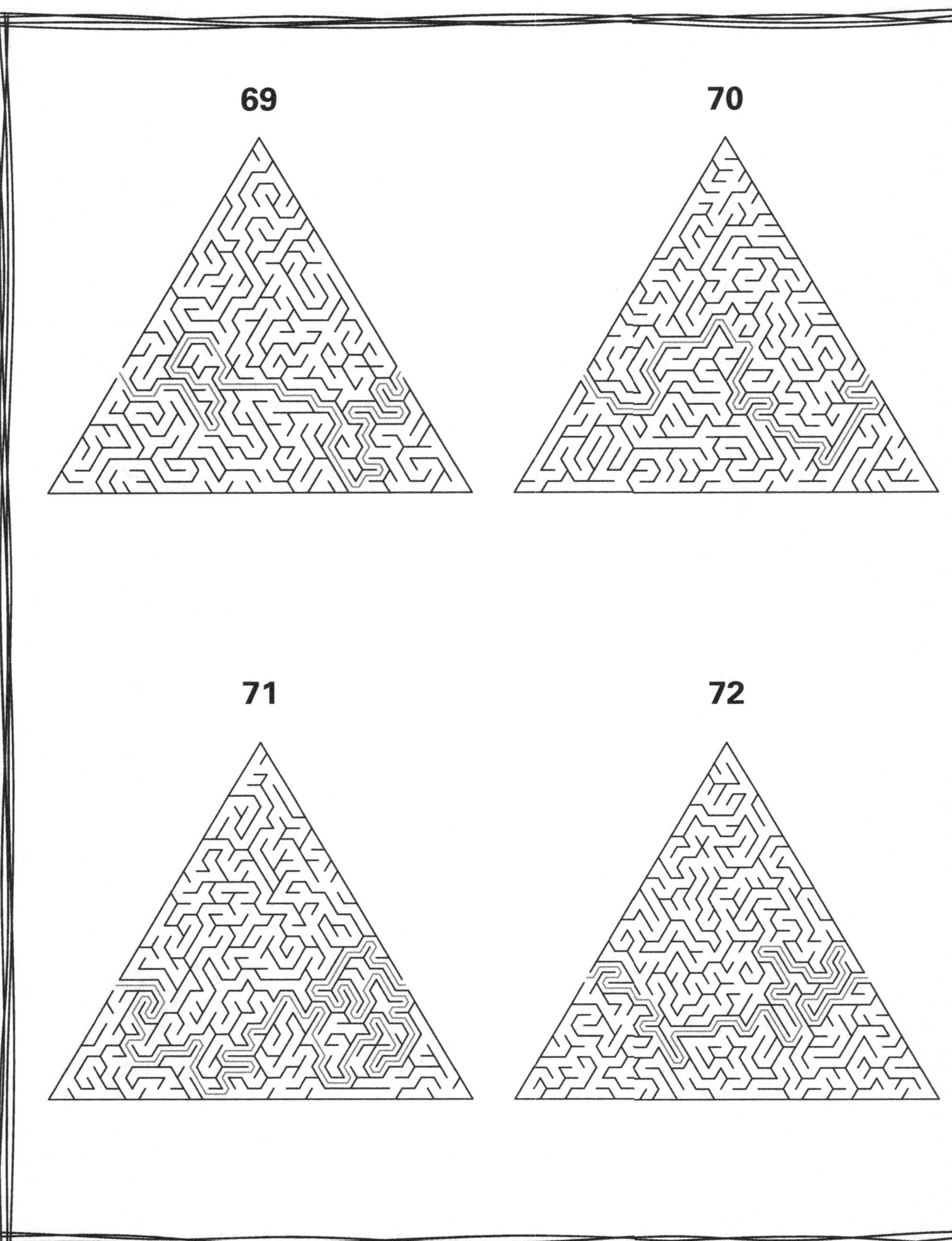
69
70
71
72

73

74

75

76

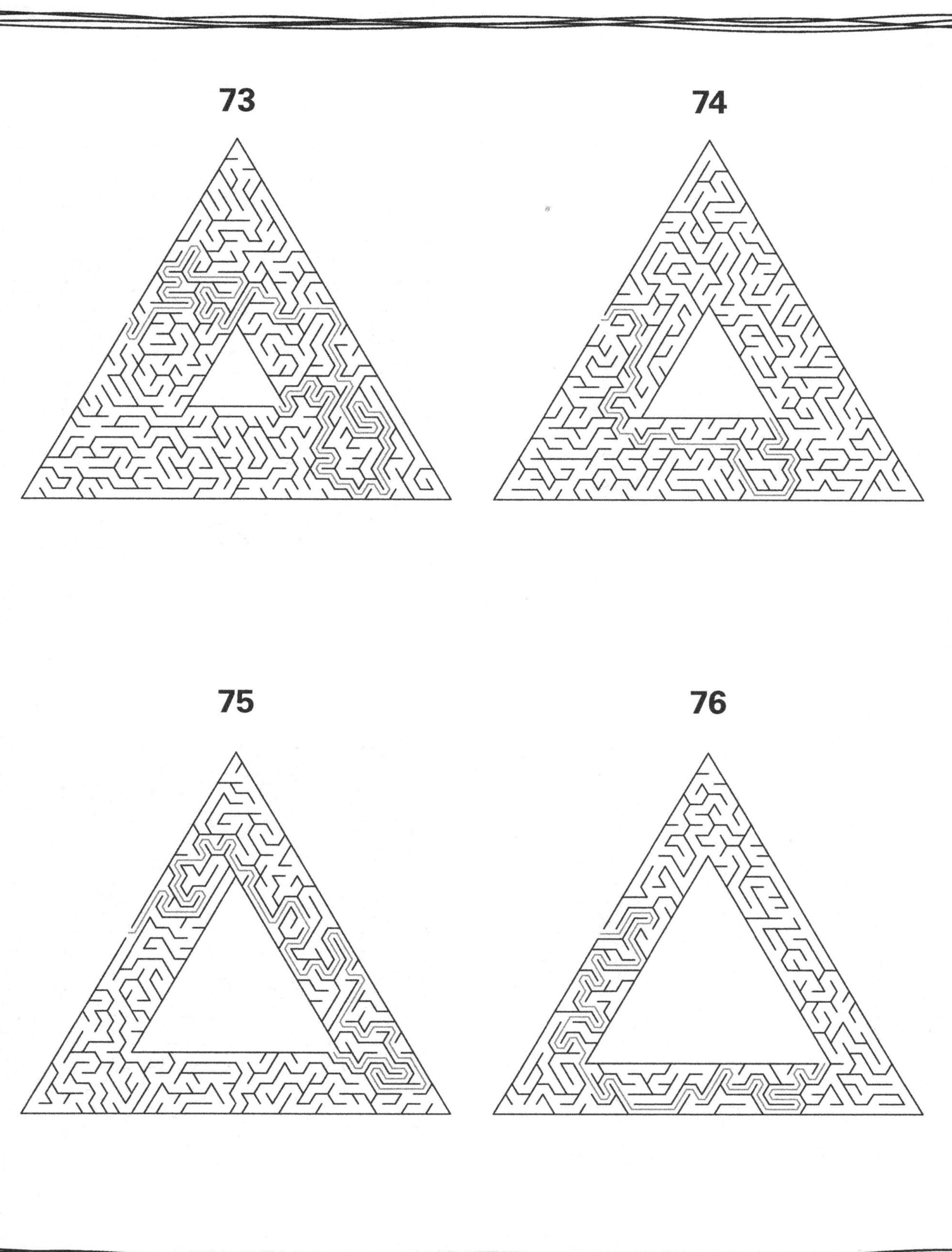

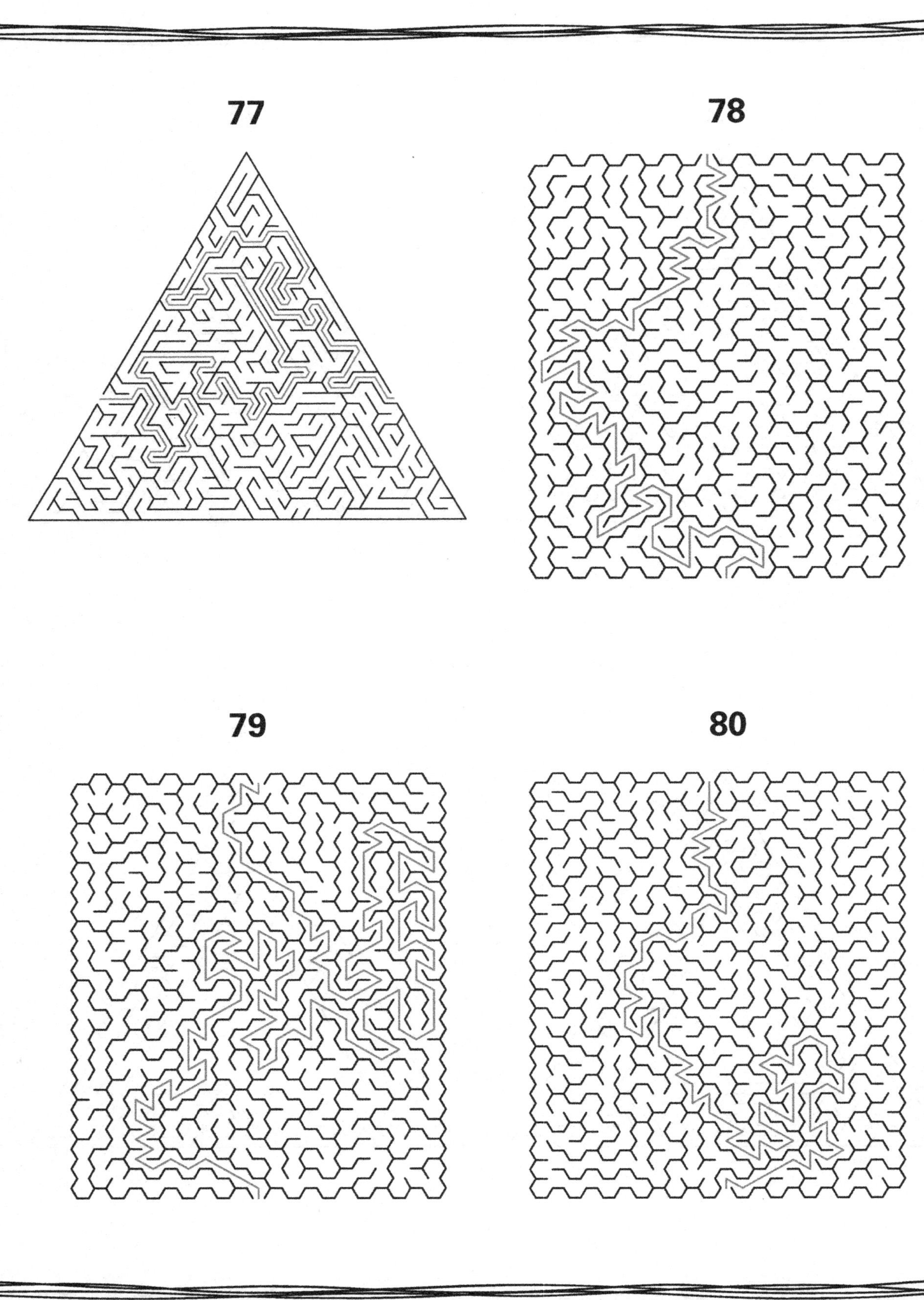

77
78
79
80

81

82

Made in the USA
Monee, IL
07 July 2026